Plateaus

by Sheila Anderson

first step nonfiction

Lerner Publications Company · Minneapolis

What is a **plateau?**

It is a kind of **landform.**

A plateau is a raised, flat piece of land.

It is higher than the land around it.

Rain and wind break away
the land around a plateau.

The sides of the plateau can be **steep.**

A plateau can be high like
a **mountain.**

Or it can be low like a hill.

Some plateaus are in the **desert.** The land is dry.

Other plateaus are covered
with green plants.

Animals live on plateaus.

Plants grow on plateaus.

People live on plateaus.

They climb plateaus.

There are many things to
do on a plateau.

Would you like to explore
a plateau?

The Roof of the World

The world's biggest and highest plateau is the Tibetan Plateau. It is located in Asia. Because it is so high, people sometimes call the Tibetan Plateau "the roof of the world."

Some of Asia's largest rivers begin in the Tibetan Plateau. These rivers provide water for millions of people.

Plateau Facts

 Plateaus are large areas of raised, flat land.

 Mesas are areas of raised, flat land that are smaller than plateaus.

 The word *mesa* in Spanish means "table." Mesas are sometimes called tablelands.

 Buttes are pieces of raised, flat land that are even smaller than mesas. Buttes look like rock towers.

The word *butte* came from a French word that means "mound" or "small hill."

 In Monument Valley, Arizona, there are two buttes called East Mitten and West Mitten because they look like giant stone mittens (with thumbs) sticking up out of the earth.

 You can see desert plateaus, mesas, and buttes in the southwest region of the United States.

Glossary

 desert – a dry area in which few plants or animals live

 landform – a natural feature of the earth's surface

 mountain – an area of land that rises to a great height

 plateau – an area of flat land that is higher than the land around it

 steep – rising or falling sharply

Index

animals – 12

desert – 10, 21

hill – 9

mountain – 8

people – 14, 15, 19

plants – 11, 13

The photographs in this book are reproduced with the permission of: © Lonely Planet Images/Getty Images, pp. 2, 3, 22 (second from top, second from bottom); © Olivier Martel/CORBIS, p. 4; © Stockbyte/Getty Images, p. 5; © Michael Nichols/National Geographic/Getty Images, p. 6; © Steven Rothfeld/Stone/Getty Images, pp. 7, 22 (bottom); © Chris Sanders/Stone/Getty Images, pp. 8, 22 (middle); © Michael Crockett Photography/The Image Bank/Getty Images, p. 9; © Norbert Rosing/ National Geographic/Getty Images, pp. 10, 22 (top); © James P. Blair/National Geographic/Getty Images, p. 11; © Daniel J. Cox/CORBIS, p. 12; © Panoramic Images/Getty Images, p. 13; © Mark A. Leman/Stone/Getty Images, p. 14; © Jose Azel/Aurora/Getty Images, p. 15; © Laura Ciapponi/Photonica/Getty Images, p. 16; © Curtis Martin/Lonely Planet Images/Getty Images, p. 17; © Gina Corrigan/Robert Harding World Imagery/Getty Images, p. 18.

Front Cover: © Gina Corrigan/Robert Harding World Imagery/Getty Images.

Lerner Publications Company
A division of Lerner Publishing Group, Inc.
241 First Avenue North
Minneapolis, MN 55401 U.S.A.

Website address: www.lernerbooks.com

Library of Congress Cataloging-in-Publication Data

Anderson, Sheila.
    Plateaus / by Sheila Anderson.
       p.   cm. — (First step nonfiction. Landforms)
    Includes index.
    ISBN: 978–0–8225–8592–3 (lib. bdg. : alk. paper)
    1. Plateaus — Juvenile literature. 2. Upland ecology — Juvenile literature. I. Title.
  GB571.A53 2008
  551.43'4 — dc22   2007007822

Manufactured in the United States of America
1 2 3 4 5 6 – DP – 13 12 11 10 09 08